*Square House Ruin
in Mystery Valley*

This map lays out the territory of Monument Valley to give you a perspective of the different sites as we journey photographically through this extraordinary terrain.

Thankfully, this precious territory remains for the most part intact, because the land was declared an Indian reservation in the late 1800's. The Indian culture honors nature in a way that the "white man" cannot yet seem to embrace fully. Many responsible people of all ethnic backgrounds are champions of land preservation over development, but the almighty dollar still reigns as a prevalent temptation of compromise even for those who perhaps would other-wise be strong.

Together we will explore MONUMENT VALLEY, land of spectacular rock formations, clear blue skies and the colorful Navajo Indian heritage. Here you will see pinnacles towering 900 feet above the valley floor, beautiful sand-stone arches, and ancient Ruins. Along this trail, we will discover the legendary Canyon de Chelly (pronounced "De Shay") considered by many the most beautiful of all

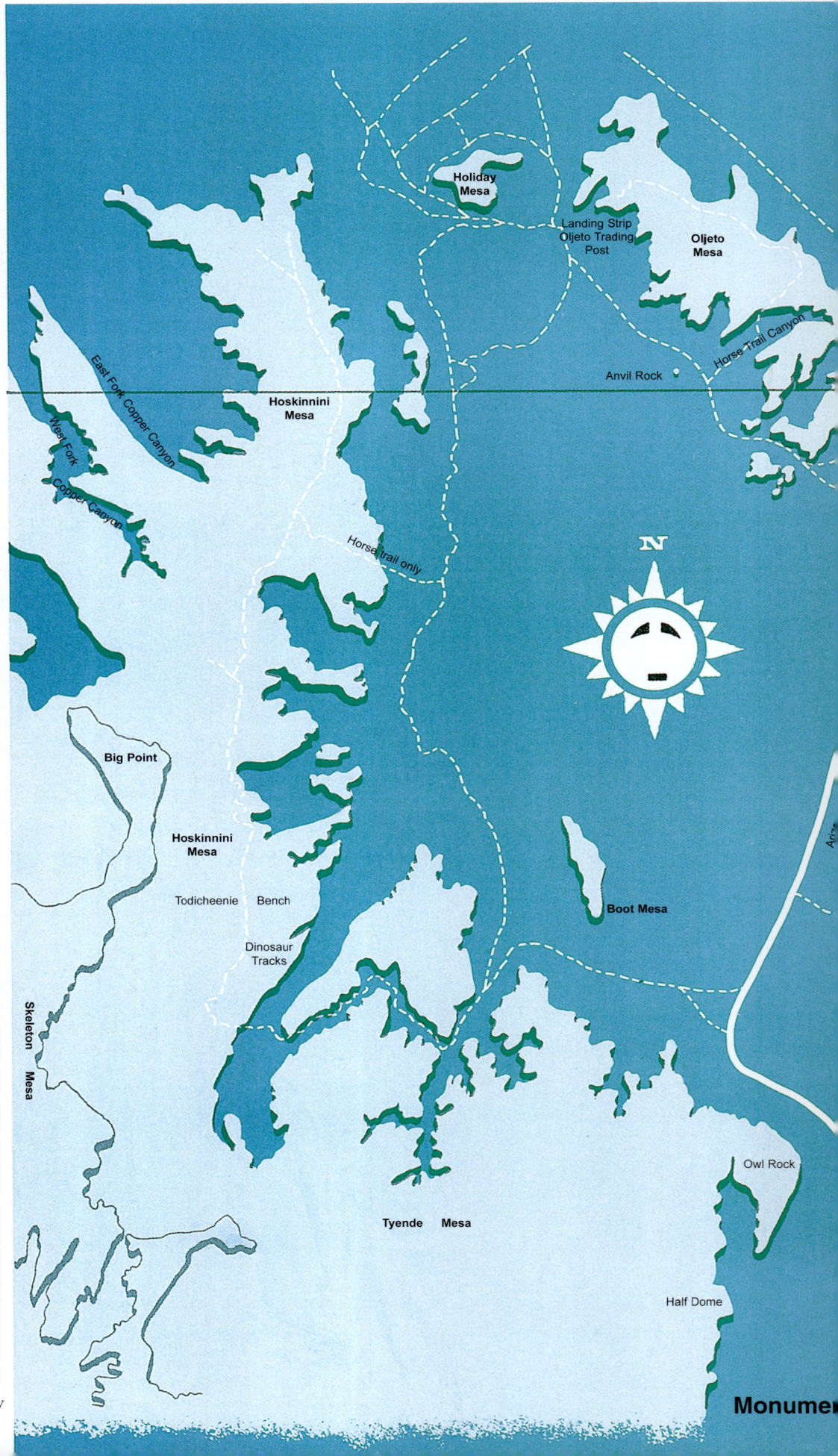

Holiday Mesa

Landing Strip
Oljeto Trading Post

Oljeto Mesa

Horse Trail Canyon

Anvil Rock

East Fork Copper Canyon

West Fork

Copper Canyon

Hoskinnini Mesa

Horse trail only

N

Big Point

Hoskinnini Mesa

Boot Mesa

Todicheenie   Bench

Dinosaur Tracks

Skeleton Mesa

Owl Rock

Tyende   Mesa

Half Dome

Monumer

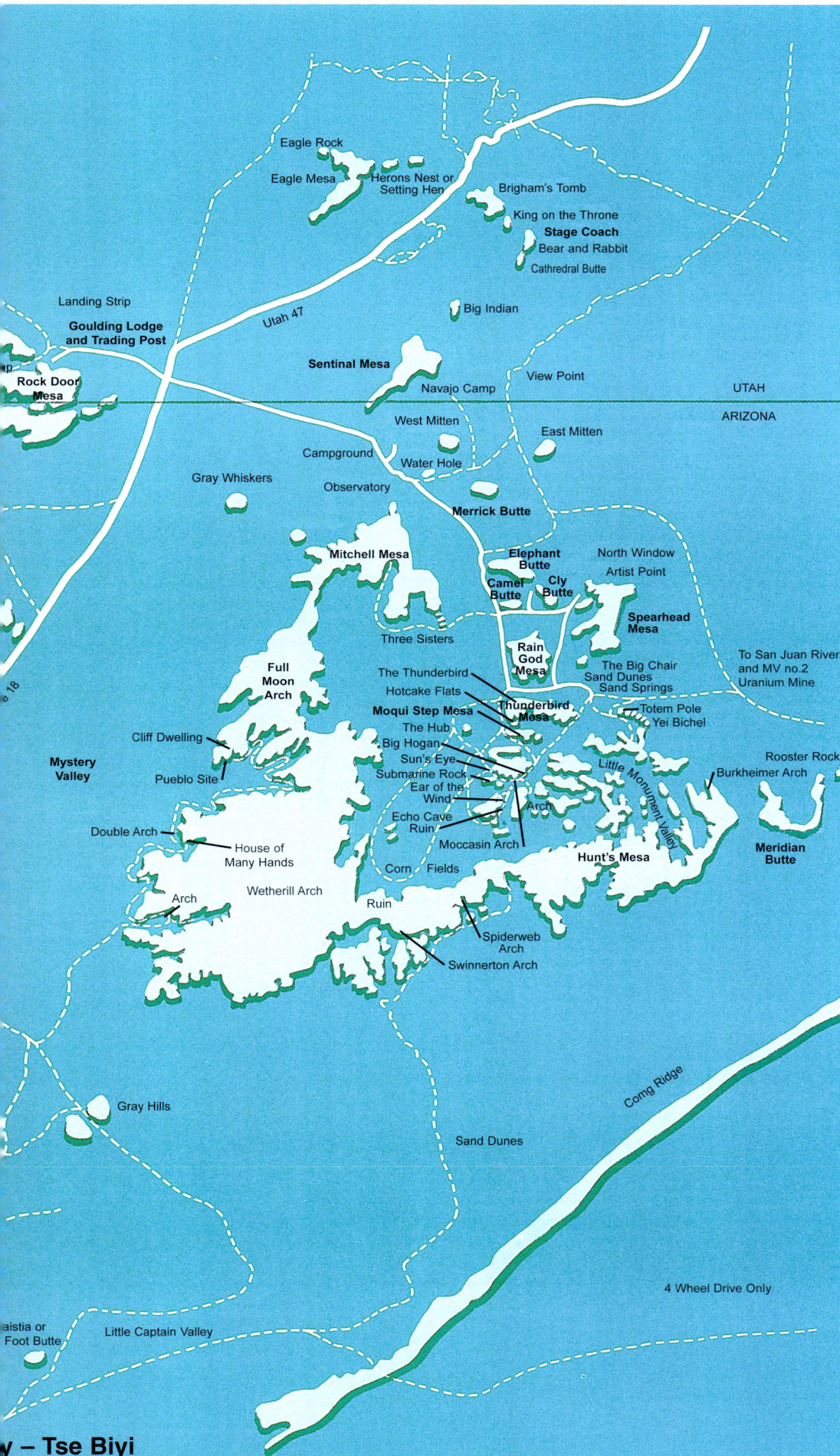

Eagle Rock

Eagle Mesa

Herons Nest or Setting Hen

Brigham's Tomb

King on the Throne

Stage Coach

Bear and Rabbit

Cathedral Butte

Landing Strip

Goulding Lodge and Trading Post

Utah 47

Big Indian

Rock Door Mesa

Sentinal Mesa

Navajo Camp

View Point

UTAH

ARIZONA

West Mitten

East Mitten

Campground

Water Hole

Gray Whiskers

Observatory

Merrick Butte

Mitchell Mesa

Elephant Butte

North Window

Artist Point

Camel Butte

Cly Butte

Three Sisters

Spearhead Mesa

Full Moon Arch

The Thunderbird

Hotcake Flats

Rain God Mesa

The Big Chair

Sand Dunes

Sand Springs

To San Juan River and MV no.2 Uranium Mine

Moqui Step Mesa

Thunderbird Mesa

Totem Pole

Yei Bichel

Cliff Dwelling

The Hub

Big Hogan

Sun's Eye

Mystery Valley

Pueblo Site

Submarine Rock

Ear of the Wind

Little Monument Valley

Rooster Rock

Burkheimer Arch

Double Arch

Echo Cave Ruin

Arch

House of Many Hands

Moccasin Arch

Hunt's Mesa

Meridian Butte

Arch

Wetherill Arch

Corn Fields

Ruin

Spiderweb Arch

Swinnerton Arch

Comg Ridge

Gray Hills

Sand Dunes

aistia or Foot Butte

Little Captain Valley

4 Wheel Drive Only

y – Tse Biyi

canyons in the country. Canyon de Chelly is a world of its own. Many miles of this scenic wonderland may be explored on the Canyon floor. Sheer rock walls rise 500 to 1000 feet high along its length. Rock towers and fantastic formations amaze you at every turn. Prehistoric Indian Ruins are everywhere leaving a trail to the past rich with mystery and unexplained phenomenon. Approximately 700 sites can be explored in Canyon de Chelly National Monument

Historians believe that the Anasazi, Hopi and Navajo people occupied the dwellings found in the canyon for about 2000 years. To these formations, 2000 years by comparison is a mere moment in a 24-hour day. The cliff dwellings are believed to have been built from A.D. 1100 to A.D. 1300. Until about A.D. 1300, the Anasazi lived among the eroded rock structures when they mysteriously vanished. Next, the Hopi, thought to be their descendents, occupied the territory until A.D. 1700. Finally, the Navajo took over and inhabit the region today.

A lone automobile travels the Monument Valley Highway. A Navajo woman and her young sons move their livestock along on the barren terrain. The Burnt Foot Rock formation in the background is unusual in that it is made of black lava stone. On the left, is the famous Agathlan Peak also known as El Capitan near Kayenta, Arizona.

Overlooking Monument
Valley Navajo Tribal Park

Navajo horses call the Canyon their home

Navajo Women heading for the Trading Post to purchase supplies

Monument Tse Biyi
(pronounced Say Be Ge)

Located on the Arizona-Utah border, this spectacular valley is one of the most remote areas in America. These photographs, taken in the mid 1960's, are lost moments of history captured forever on these pages. They record a time in the Navajo Nation when Native American families tended their flocks, lived in dwellings of logs and mud called hogans, made their world renowned craft work and lived a simple lifestyle in nature. Today, the modernization of their culture has left their faithful horses in the dust of their pick up trucks along with their native dress and natural habitats. These treasured photographs document a part of our American Heritage that once was and will never be again. With this we hope that, should you travel to these magical locations yourself, the echo of these pages will be recalled as you visit these places today.

This opening photograph is of Everett Mann with his horse. Both have long since traveled to the spirit world, yet their presence remains like guardians of another time, dressed in the beginnings of cultural transition, a blending of their conqueror's clothing with their own native flair.

Red Lake Homesite

These Navajo women are gathered in front of this typical Indian hogan. Emma Shorty is in the foreground. From left to right are Louise Claw, Helen Boone, Dolly Turquoise, and Julia Turquoise.

(right) Dolly and Julia Turquoise are on their way to their homesite at Red Lake.

(opposite page) Betatakin Ruin, at Navajo National Monument, was built in a natural cavern cradle in this monolithic wonder.

Betatakin Ruin

Navajo Guide, Eddie Austin, relaxes after his journey to Betatakin Ruin in Navajo National Monument. Keet Seal Ruin (not shown) is in the same canyon 8 miles northwest of this site. This well preserved village seen in this photograph was rich with activity as the Anasazi people went about their daily routine so many years ago. Anasazi means "The Ancient Ones" in the Navajo language. Remnants of their culture are scattered throughout the four corners region. The classic perception of Indians living only in teepees is less than accurate as these dwellings demonstrate. Their choice to utilize nature's protective formations enhanced by their handiwork was both ingenious and logical.

These cliff dwellings protected them from the elements and their enemies. Speculations remain as to who their enemies might have been; perhaps the early Navajo or Apache tribes. One of the most fascinating mysteries about the Anasazi culture is their quick disappearance. Some believe it was due to weather changes affecting their ability to grow corn, beans and squash, which was the main staple food. Others wonder of things unknown that caused them to simply vanish.

Alice Yazzie, a beautiful young Navajo maiden, donned her finest jewelry to adorn her native dress as she posed for this photograph with her buckskin horse.

The Tsegi Trading Post

The Tseqi Trading Post near Kayenta, Arizona supplied the necessities of life to residents in a twenty mile radius. The photograph below is a two family log hogan built directly across the street from the trading post. Here we see the traditional cradle boards, which kept the babies safe and secure.

Herding their Flock

Two Navajo women herd their sheep and goats near Monument Valley's famous Yei-bet-chai and Totem Pole formations. The stark terrain requires that they keep their flock moving to find food and water, both of which are scarce in this valley.

Hunt's Mesa

Cly Butte is named after the Cly family, one of most famous families of Monument Valley. Actually, the name "Cly" is a white man's corruption of "Claw", his given Indian name. Grandfather Cly, who was one of the early Navajos in the area, lies buried at the North Window (the viewpoint overlooking the North part of Monument Valley). The personal belongings of Hosteen Cly (his saddle, shovels, axe, coffee pot, pans, etc.) were laid on the ground over his grave and remained there until about 1950 when they were carried off by vandals. His descendants are still living in this part of the valley.

Hosteen Cly's son, Willie, has been photographed more than any other Navajo on the Reservation. Willie is on the cover and is seen throughout this book along with other members of his family. Here, high on the edge of Hunt's Mesa, Willie Cly and Suzie Yazzie overlook the area called Little Monument Valley.

High on the edge of Hunt's Mesa, Willy Cly and Suzie Yazzie overlook the area called Little Monument Valley

Willie and his daughter rest with the
vast view of Monument Valley as
a backdrop behind them.

The Cly Family Hogan

The Cly family set up shelter near the Three Sisters Formation. To the right, they built a winter hogan with a cedar pole frame, which is covered with mud. A hole in the middle of the roof is left for the smoke to escape from their fire, which they use to cook as well as to keep warm in cold seasons. On the left, a summer shelter made from poles and brush is used in the heat of summer.

The Famous Navajo Weaving

Willy Cly looks on as his daughter weaves in
front of their hogan on a hot summer day.

Willie Cly drives his herd in the winter snow

Totem Pole and Yei-bet-chai Dancers

These slender rock formations stand against a rich, cloudy sky.
In the distance on the far left, rests Rooster Rock.

John Cly and his horse

John Cly, Willie's brother, is poised on a rock formation against a clear blue sky.

The Cly family tending their flock

It was often customary that the Navajo man would ride his horse as the woman walked when they moved their sheep to another pasture. Notice Hunt's Mesa, Totem Pole and Yei-bet-chai Dancers deep in the background in the upper right corner.

The horse seen in these two photographs was killed by a bolt of lightning. The rider lived to tell the story, but a short time later met his demise by entering a sweat lodge after imbibing too much alcohol.

Sunset at the Cly family hogan

The only mode of transportation, other than their horses, was the wagon seen in the foreground. Hunt's Mesa is the large formation in the background. The single spire in the center is once again the Totem Pole with the Yei-bet-chai Dancers just to the left. A baby and a young boy patiently watch as their mother carefully weaves the magic of her craft on the hand loom in the late afternoon sun.

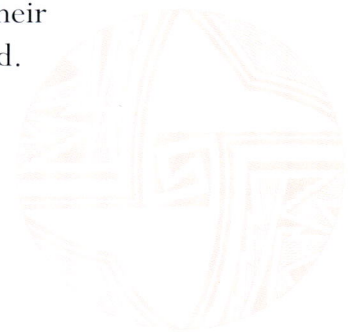

Jeddito Sand Springs

Water is scarce and precious in this beautiful, barren terrain. Here, the livestock is driven to one of the few water holes to quench their thirst at Jeddito Sand Springs.

Mitten Rock

A young native girl rides her pony about a quarter mile from Mitten Rock.

The Navajo Culture

These following pages capture tender moments of the Navajo culture. Trusted friend and valuable worker is the sheep dog seen with a young Navajo girl. These dogs both protected against wild animals and helped herd the goats and sheep. The wool from the sheep was an intrinsic part of the culture for the magnificent woven blankets the Navajo people are still so famous for creating.

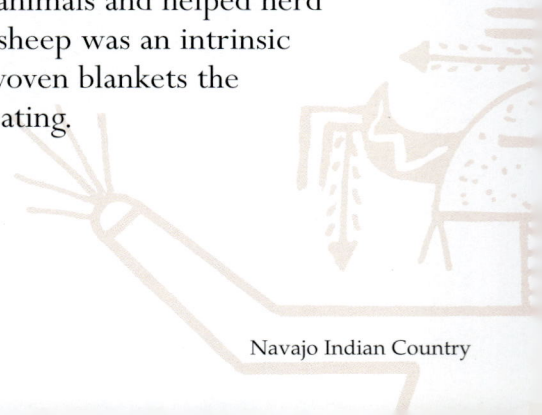

One Generation Teaches Another

This family grouping demonstrates a typical day in the tradition of the Navajo culture during this era. The grandmother weaves, teaching her granddaughter this native craft. The animals are an integrated part of the family structure. The young girl plays with her puppy and looks after her younger brother.

White House Ruin

*T*his is a closer view of White House Ruin in the colorful beauty of autumn.

At the time when this was originally built, the Anasazi culture was a rather peaceful existence. Later, the Navajo and Apache tribes were more aggressive in nature. Finally, the white man changed the culture entirely with their oppressive force early in the 1800's.

On April 1, 1931, Canyon de Chelly National Monument was established. Over 130 square miles of land are preserved here. The Navajo Nation owns the land and the park is operated for the public in cooperation with the National Park Service and the Navajo people. Only Navajo guides are permitted on the property. It is, after all, a nation within our nation separated by a treaty with the United States so many years ago.

These vast views taken from Rim Rock show the amazing perspective.
Above, White House Ruin is a tiny spot on the left wall.
A wash gracefully meanders through the floor of the canyon below this ruin.

White House Ruin in Summer

Perhaps the most treasured Indian Ruin in the country, White House Ruin, is visited by thousands of appreciative spectators every year.

The following page shows a breathtaking view of Spider Rock. These formations are made of sandstone and were formed by endless years of erosion…a sculpture of divine mystery. It is difficult to distinguish a profile of importance from one site to another. They stand as world wonders that beckon to our spirit giving us a taste of timelessness… ancient and otherworldly. These surreal masterpieces of nature dwarf any human effort that we might hope to realize.

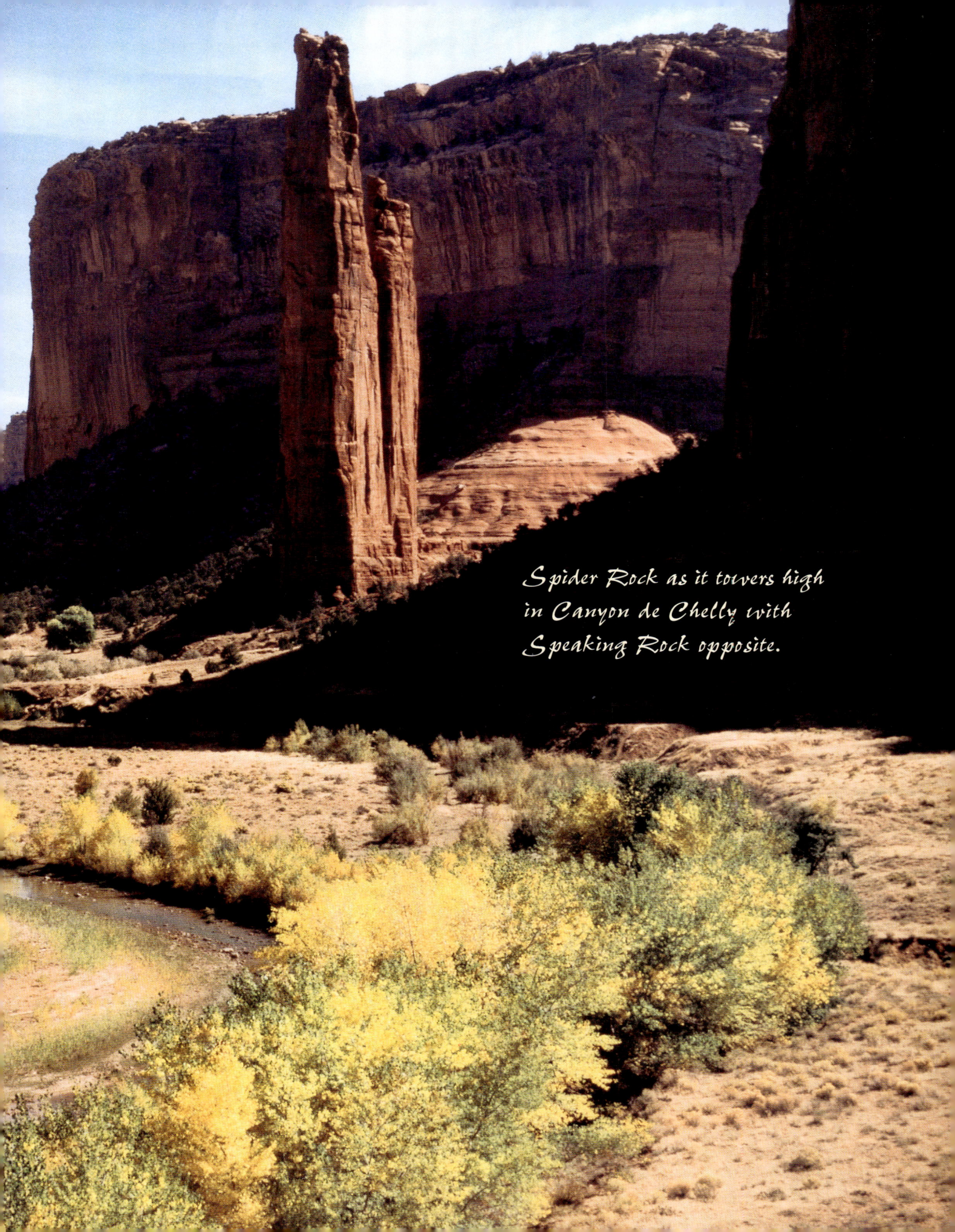

Spider Rock as it towers high in Canyon de Chelly with Speaking Rock opposite.

Nomad's Land

As the season changes, another Navajo is driving his herd of horses
out of the canyon for the winter.

(Left) This family has loaded up their wagon and is leaving the canyon for the winter.
The deep snow is too difficult for them to sustain themselves. A slow cultural transition
begins as this wagon is fitted with old automobile tires instead of the traditional wooden
wagon wheels.

Navajo Indian Country

Winter In Monument Valley

High up on Artist's Point, capturing the snow on a winter day in December is often rare.
Snow melts in a matter of days in this country. Central Monument Valley rests in the background.

Here at Centennial Mesa, sheep paw through the snow to find food after a snowfall.

Moccasin Arch

A Navajo woman and her daughter enjoy a ride
in front of Moccasin Arch in Monument Valley.

Standing Cow Ruin

Johnny Aguerra, who was the most famous and knowledgeable guide in his time, stands observing this spectacular ancient art known as Standing Cow Ruin. Johnny guided people through these ancient sites for over twenty years.